# IN DEFENSE OF MISFORTUNE

Riya Aarini

*In Defense of Misfortune*

Text copyright © 2022 by Riya Aarini

This is a work of fiction. Names, characters, businesses, places, events, locales, and incidents are either the products of the author's imagination or used in a fictitious manner. Any resemblance to actual persons, living or dead, or actual events is purely coincidental.

ISBN: 978-1-956496-11-6 (Paperback)

ISBN: 978-1-956496-12-3 (eBook)

Library of Congress Control Number: 2022916384

First published in Austin, Texas, USA

Visit www.riyapresents.com

# CONTENTS

# CONTENTS

## ON MY MONIKER

I may be known as misfortune, but I'm Mr. Misfortune
to you. Show elders some respect. I've been around
since time began, and I deserve to be treated with
some level of veneration. But do I get that? No! I'm
simultaneously cursed every time my name is brought
up. Complicating matters is my archnemesis, Lady
Fortune, who somehow gets a glorious title before her
name. Why does she get a splendiferous title? I don't get
even a remotely dignified one. I'm just referred to as a
common noun, of all things, not even anything that's
officially considered a formal name—one deserving of
a capital letter at the start. There's nothing flattering

1

about being dismissively discussed as a noun of all things. This whole name issue kind of makes me feel worthless, like I'm unwanted in people's lives.

## ON BEING AN UNAPPRECIATED TEACHER

I share a lot of commonalities with teachers, educators, instructors of impressionable minds. Like teachers, I provide a valuable service to the students of life. Also like teachers, I feel I'm grossly undervalued. Most people would never learn about the truths of life without my help. Where would you be without a lesson in humility or forgiveness or patience? In fact, my contributions to humanity are quite extensive: I influence perspectives; I shape minds; I guide actions. Would you ever graduate from the school of life without me teaching you a thing or two? Listen, I pride myself on disseminating life-changing wisdom to folks at all stages of life; and I continue providing my priceless service, despite being classed as an underrated teacher. School may be out for a brief vacation, folks, but this teacher's always in, preparing to deliver up an unexpected life lesson or two. But do I get a thank-you? Mostly never.

## ON WORKING WITH MY ARCHNEMESIS

You may not realize it, but rivals, like Lady Fortune and myself, sometimes operate in tandem. It's a pain to work together with my archnemesis, but that's the way it is—my bad luck, you could say. You see, depending on the time and place, Lady Fortune may make an initial appearance, and I enter the picture later. At other times, I arrive first, and she follows. It's a delicate dance between us. It's not uncommon for life on earth to be visited by both of us—one after the other, that is. No matter how you look at it, though, we're never in the same place at the same time. Since no one knows which one of us is destined to precede the other, we're as unpredictable as the weather. Not knowing the weather can be darn uncomfortable. So always be prepared for either of us—and carry an extra sweater wherever you go.

## ON THE LATE AIRPLANE PASSENGER

It's kind of hard to imagine something as inexplicable as me until I pay you a personal visit. So I'm here to give you an example of how Lady Fortune and I work. You may be familiar with this story, but it's worth repeating for the sake of example. One fine day in a busy city in an arid corner of the earth, a woman in her midlife hailed a taxi to the airport. "Get me to the airport, quickly," she said. "I've got my daughter's thirtieth birthday party to attend." The taxi driver hurried, but I stalled the cab in the middle of heavy traffic. "My plane's about to take off. Hurry it up, you fool!" the woman yelled. The taxi driver slammed his foot on the gas but, thanks to me, had nowhere to go in the jungle of cars surrounding his. Wide-eyed, the woman stared out to see her plane take off. She cursed the taxi driver a million times over. "I've missed my plane, you idiot!" She banged on the seat. As she looked out of the window of the cab, she witnessed her plane take a nosedive and crash, instantly killing everyone on board in a burst of flames. She gawked at the scene with her jaw dropped. This is where my part ends and Lady Fortune's begins. The woman's initial moment of shock was followed by exhilarating joy. "You saved my life!" she yelled to the taxi driver. She hugged the driver and unloaded a stack of bills into his hand. The woman was alive to attend her daughter's thirty-first birthday party, and the overjoyed taxi driver was able to buy a brand-new cab with the generous tip he earned. Now that's one of the many mysterious ways Lady Fortune and I work together.

## ON BEING EVERYWHERE

I'm omnipresent. I'm universal. I'm ubiquitous. Get it? I'm everywhere. There's no escaping me when I strike. I hit every form of life on earth, from the rubber trees in the rainforests to the viperfish at the darkest depths of the oceans to the gazelles and blue wildebeests freely roaming the savannas. Even your darling houseplant is not immune; when your blushing philodendron becomes infested with sap-sucking mealybugs and starts to hopelessly wilt, guess who's made a visit? I'm as pervasive as the air you breathe. I've visited every continent on earth many times over. Famine, drought, natural calamities—they're all the consequences of a visit from yours truly. Hey, I can't help it. It's just my nature to deliver hard luck. I'm unlike my archrival, Lady Fortune, who shows up only on rare occasions. That means everyone gets a taste of me at some point and to some degree. I'm not off limits to anyone! You're welcome.

## ON THE REJECTED MEDICAL RESIDENT

I enjoy the freedom of showing up in people's lives whenever I please. Unfortunately for me, Lady Fortune follows the exact same methodology and outdoes everything I do. Let me illustrate with the story of an ambitious third-year medical student. Ever since Matt was five years old, he wanted to be a doctor. What kind of doctor? Well, in medical school, he decided his specialty would be ophthalmology. He prepared himself for a life as a skilled eye doctor, one who studies vision like a hawk studies the open meadows. Matt applied for his first choice, a top-tier residency program in ophthalmology, but because of my meddling, he was rejected. He applied to his second and third ophthalmology residency choices; but again, he was met with rejections. He-he! I'm kind of underhanded, I admit. Matt went home with knots in his stomach. Locking himself in his darkened bedroom for days, he entertained ideations of going to some ophthalmology heaven. Then Lady Fortune comes along and steals my spotlight. The nerve! Matt collected himself and applied for residency in a far different specialty: pediatrics. He was instantly accepted. It was during his enlightening three-year pediatric residency that he met the love of his life, another pediatrics resident training in the same program. The perfectly compatible doctors got married and eventually started a family. With a loving wife, a healthy child, and a rewarding career, Matt felt he was the happiest man in the field of medicine; not a day went by that he didn't thank his lucky stars. But if it weren't for me getting in the way of his professional aspirations, I dare say he'd have been one lonely and miserable ophthalmologist.

## ON ADVENTURE

Come on, you've got to admit that I shake life up a bit. Without me, your life would be unbearably picture perfect—and dreadfully boring. I'm the hot sauce on your pineapple pizza, the monster storm cloud menacing over the Everest base camp, the thin lake ice under your skates. I promise excitement, relief from the humdrum of every expectation being immediately fulfilled. When I show up, you'll find yourself jumping three-foot hurdles or winding through mazes of obstacles that even the finest prizewinning cocker spaniel in the national dog show would find utterly bewildering. I add zest to living. Consider that you're the whitewater rafter, and I'm the raging river. You navigate carefully to avoid tipping over in your kayak or crashing into a sharp-edged boulder jutting out haphazardly from beneath the surface of the foaming white water. Try to accept some encouragement from yours truly, who's seen it all, from greater to lesser battles: when you eventually make it out of the furious rapids, you'll have earned the meritorious badge to dignifiedly hold your head a little higher.

## ON BEING UNPREDICTABLE

When you get a dose of me, you'll never know what's in store—that's how unpredictable I am. I don't adhere to a special formula. I mean, no two unfortunate events are ever alike. Similarities may exist, but I can't replicate myself 100 percent all of the time. Plus, I don't follow a calendar or a schedule. I just make an entrance when the circumstances are right. That makes me somewhat erratic. See, I'm the mystery flavor in your premium coffee: caramel, amaretto, or pumpkin spice—except these are delightful flavors to most palates. I tend to be a little less desirable. No one ever orders a cup of licorice-flavored misfortune embellished with squiggly latte art before heading for the rigors of the morning workday. Regardless of how or when we meet, I deliver the jolt to wake you up from your mind-numbing existence.

## ON WINNING THE LOTTERY

Matching the six winning numbers in the Mega Millions lottery jackpot seems like a distant dream—until it becomes a fateful reality, and I unexpectedly stride in. See, winning the lottery is a once-in-a-lifetime event, one that I especially like inviting myself into. It's an instance when Lady Fortune makes her initial visit, and, to the shock of the nouveau riche, I show up much later. There's a lot for me to play with when it comes to doing what I do best—delivering hard luck to the lucky. Having barely taken a breath after claiming their winnings, lottery winners still dazed about their windfall squander their newfound gazillions. Within the blink of an eye, divorce looms, gambling debts mount, and the first-available hit man is contracted—and these amusing aspects of life are due solely to an investment of my creative efforts. Don't forget that I also connect you with overgreedy long-lost relatives, you know, the ones who never acknowledged your existence until they heard through the family grapevine—specifically, their tenth cousin, twice removed—that you struck gold in the state lottery.

## ON THE PHILOSOPHY STUDENT WHO GOT DUMPED

I work in incomprehensible ways. Let me elaborate with the most interesting account of a philosophy student. In his last year in a renowned philosophy program at a prestigious university, Nathaniel invested himself in a romantic relationship with a second-year student. Flippant and flighty, the young woman gave her heart to another man, dumping Nathaniel in the course of one short afternoon. I played my role well, as was clear, sending an arrow of sorrow where sorrow is due. Despite my efforts, Lady Fortune had alternate plans for him. Saddened but no longer tethered to romantic ideals, Nathaniel felt free to pursue the truest love of his life and joined a monastery. Within its walls, the newly graduated philosophy student flourished as a monk. In time, the young man started giving teachings around the world, earning recognition and praise from supporters. Looking back on his earlier heartache, Nathaniel felt quite pleased with his current situation, going so far as to tremble at the thought of having narrowly escaped being tied down to a nagging wife, three naughty kids, and a burdensome mortgage. As a monk, he was as free and happy as a songbird. Surely, you must agree that I made significant contributions to his life choices, with Lady Fortune handling the rest with characteristic ease. Spreading a bit of myself around isn't so bad, now, is it?

## ON BITTERNESS

I realize a visit from me may leave you feeling bitter, and you want to take out your anger on anything that moves. But don't lose your perspective because of me. Instead, I wholeheartedly recommend replacing your resentment with respect—and this is coming from someone who's been around the block, oh, an infinite number of times. Is that so hard? Respecting members of our estimable society should be a piece of cake. After all, it was clever folks who invented, designed, and manufactured the life conveniences that everyone holds so dear. Without the ingenuity of others, would you have all-terrain four-wheelers, loaded cheese fries, or indoor plumbing? I think not! Life would be extra hard without the glories of modern amenities. So open your mind, look around, and have some appreciation for the little things that make life rewarding. And quit blaming me for your persistent bitterness.

## ON EQUALITY

I pride myself on being exceptionally fair. I don't discriminate in any way whatsoever. Whether you're rich or poor, male or female, young or old, green or purple—I make it my intention to pay you a visit. See, I value everyone equally. Folks with high social status, an impressive education, or notable income are likewise as important to me as anyone whom Lady Fortune has never visited yet. I'll hit up any Tom, Dick, or Susanna, when the time comes. Indeed, I'm that open minded. The truth is, I think most folks wouldn't mind me being a little partial. It'd keep me away from some of them, at least; and, for them, that's a relief. But I've got standards, and I aim to continue abiding by the highest laws of the land. There'll never be anyone in our great world who can justifiably call me biased, because my personal motto is that everyone of all scruples is important to me and could warrant a visit at any time. Yep, you stand to benefit when you take cues about fair-mindedness from me.

## ON SHALLOW POCKETS

I'm no fish out of water, so let me share with you a
story about the way I operate in the scheme of life.
Jasmine was as poor as a church mouse. She couldn't
afford a three-pound bag of tangerines, a weekday
afternoon at the local roller rink, or new shoes. In
fact, her shoes were raggedy, worn to the sole, and two
sizes too small. Thanks to me, she knew the meaning
of hardship. Then one day Lady Fortune showed up in
her life and helped her land a lucrative job. The young
woman suddenly found herself with deep enough
pockets to buy the fanciest shoes for herself, her whole
family, and then some. Jasmine, never forgetting where

she came from, started a nonprofit in her hometown called New Shoes for Old Souls. She made sure everyone in her neighborhood had a comfy pair of shoes that fit just right. Now that's something to write home about. But circling back to me. Would she ever have developed a magnanimous spirit of generosity toward the less fortunate if it weren't for me interfering in her early days? Listen, I may have an inglorious reputation for spreading misery, but there's always a good reason behind doing what I do. Make no qualms about it: I'm as life changing as Lady Fortune.

## ON BEING LIKE A VIRUS

I admit, I need a host to survive. That makes me similar to a virus, like the common cold virus or the flu virus or the coronavirus. I need you to survive so I don't have to keep searching for another viable host. That's one of the worst parts of who I am, constantly having to find hosts who'll keep me going. It's totally unpredictable whether I'll find someone suitable and to my liking. My survival is 100 percent dependent on yours, so I make sure I don't completely put you out of service. Furthermore, the reason I've been around so long is that humanity is so resilient. People have bounced back numerous times after I've appeared. Listen, without you, there's no me. Like it or not, we enjoy a symbiotic relationship. So it's important for me to leave you with a feeling of triumph or other little bit of benefit, so, like the flu virus, I can someday come around again.

## ON VIRTUES

I pride myself on inspiring the finer virtues in humanity. Humility, generosity, and understanding are just a few of the noble character traits I can boast of in my oeuvre. I am proud to say I also bring out the bravery that would otherwise be sitting idly at the bottom of your cache of personal strengths. Would you be nearly as humble if I hadn't knocked you down over and over with life challenges? Would you ever understand the troubles others go through if it weren't for me giving you the same medicine? I don't believe you'd be anywhere near as generous if I hadn't shown you what it's like to have less. You'd hardly have a chance to show your courage without little old me testing you. You understand life because I made an appearance in yours. Not everyone stands to improve after I've visited, but that's the rare few. Rather, the majority of folks grow in determination after navigating the seemingly unsurpassable obstacle course I put them through. It's not always obvious at first, but trust me. Countless times, I've personally witnessed the phoenix rising majestically from the mountainous pile of speckled-gray ashes.

## ON BRINGING PEOPLE TOGETHER

You know, I have the uncanny ability to bring people together. I'm unlike any other force on earth. I may send a fierce tornado that rips through a small town or a hurricane that tears up residential properties along the coast, bungling up people's lives in all sorts of inhospitable ways. While the devastation is immense, so is the outpouring of genuine support. Communities band together with one aim: to rebuild. There are no biases, no hee-haws; it's just humanity helping humanity out. Men and women, young and old, show their compassion by hammering nails, distributing food and water, and being there for an entire community in their time of grief. Inspiring compassion and sympathy are common threads in mostly every visit I make. It's like my signature style, my trademark, my unmistakable brand. And if folks don't lend a hand directly, they open their hearts and wallets. People from all over the world make generous donations when I send unanticipated calamities and reverberating destructions. Have you ever seen that level of immediate heartfelt support at a thousand-guest wedding or a summertime ballgame or the grand opening of a Philadelphia deli? Nope! I'm unique in my special way of bringing out the best in humanity, so don't give me the evil eye every time I appear. It's a little unnerving. See, in general, my brief encounter with folks leaves them with bigger hearts than if I'd never showed up.

## ON BEING A BEAUTIFIER

I have a far superior tactic for beautifying people than eighteen-millimeter false eyelashes, a walk-in closet bursting with the latest casual trousers, or celebrity-branded cologne and perfume. I'm even better at enhancing physical appearances than those strenuous hour-long workouts at the overpriced gym halfway across town that never leaves clean towels. And don't even get me started on diamonds and bling. You see, folks who find their way out of my grips emerge far more beautiful than even I could have ever imagined. But it's not the outer, physical beauty I'm talking about here. It's a deeper, inward beauty that radiates out of a person who's been strengthened by their grace in handling my disruptions. Rarely is this refined beauty achieved out of the blue. It's not like they can brush a wand of crimson blush across their cheeks and be considered gorgeous—which is a little over-the-top ridiculous. Rather, they've worked long and hard to overcome my trademark turmoil. Eh, even I'm humbled. *Sniffle*. Geez, these strong and beautiful folks just put me in my place sometimes.

## ON COMING AROUND MORE THAN ONCE

I tend to favor some folks. That's why I come around multiple times within the course of their lives. I just love the feeling of knowing I contributed in some small way to their strength and fortitude. If they don't bounce back after I've met with them, I don't feel too good about it. But hey, it's what comes with the territory of delivering angst on a regular basis. I win some. I lose some. I've visited some people so many times that they don't even make room for me at the gathering table anymore. It's kind of hurtful in my teary eyes, like our relationship is no longer working. I know I can be relentless, pushing my way into folks' lives. Some of them wise up and shut the door, put up barricades, install a vertical series of ten deadbolt locks—all in efforts to keep me out. I stand there scratching my head, wondering what makes me so revolting. It's times like these that I honestly feel that entering myself into acceptance and commitment therapy would have a lifesaving benefit.

## ON BOXING MATCHES

When I show up, it's you against me in the ring. I may knock you out. *TKO!* But I need you to get back up and fight. The better the fight, the bigger the reward. It doesn't even matter if you win. So don't back down when you and I are up against each other. It would leave a sour taste in the mouths of the audience that's amped up for a fight. Show them—and me— what you've got. All it takes is a few minutes of your time, three to be exact, in each round. And we've got twelve rounds to fight. I pick my opponents carefully and consider the category of fighter before I send any punches your way. If I've picked you, then you're built to handle me. Should our match end with a single power punch that knocks you out, I'll be one sore winner. See, all the fun happens when you stay in the ring and fight for as long as you can. Even when you feel like you've reached your breaking point, don't give up. That's when all the magic happens: transformation, growth, and ultimately winning. And who knows? You just might send me cowering back to the sanctuary of my sweaty fighter's corner like a droopy Irish setter with its shaggy tail between its legs.

## ON MY SPECIAL DAY

I've got my own special day, and it just tickles me pink.
In some parts of the world, it's Friday the thirteenth,
and people freak out, being on edge, attributing
every minor mishap to the dreaded day. In others, it's
Tuesday the thirteenth. Those dates are thought of as
so unlucky that people alter their behaviors, some even
refusing to shave. I'm flattered that way back when,
the number thirteen inspired the renowned Thirteen
Club; gentlemen defied superstition, purposely walking
under ladders and dining at tables with thirteen
brave guests. I'd have loved to have been invited to
enjoy a dinner conversation about the likelihood of

me coming around. I'm not limited by date or in any way whatsoever. Yet it's not uncommon for people to believe there are days that are considered even unluckier. October 29 is one example. That day in 1929 was nicknamed Black Tuesday; I sent the stock market crashing, which triggered the Great Depression. Whoa! My influence was dire, even for my standards. On a good note, I'm actually quite honored folks think so well of my impact that specific days on the calendar are reserved just for me. At least I get some respect some of the time.

## ON EXPECTATIONS

Unrealistic expectations attract me like bees to a jam sandwich. I've visited irrational folks who've expected the world to kneel down at their feet, and I've had a grand old time messing with their worldview. They just expected too much, and high expectations are notorious for inviting disappointments, unhappiness, the whole shebang. In contrast, there are those humble folks who hardly expect anything and are satisfied with the crumbs. Others are only happy when they've got the loaf in their hands. Then there are people who just demand the whole bakery—and these unrealistic folks deserve my sympathy. Unfortunately, I can't send compassion their way, because I have little of it. Instead, I deliver a hefty dose of my namesake. So, rather than drown in high expectations that'll never be fulfilled, calm down, take a deep breath, and bask in the satisfaction of the here and now. I guarantee, you'll be successful in shooing me away at that point.

## ON IMPERMANENCE

I'm not a permanent fixture in anyone's life.
Temporary is the name of my game. Gosh, I'd
be bored out of my mind if I had to be constant in
anyone's life. I need variety, which is why I show up all
over the world, in different forms and disguises, and
create all sorts of unimaginable havoc. The world is
mine for the taking. With the sole intent of avoiding
boredom, I jump from one person to the next, never
staying too long with any individual. That's just how I
roll. Too many opportunities for disorder tempt me
in my daily existence, and I aim to take advantage of
each one of them. So, you can say with certainty that

I'm as temporary as temporary gets. I'm like a seasonal warehouse associate who's only needed until the merchandise orders are processed. Once the season's done, off I go to seek new adventures and deliver the latest forms of chaos. Remember, I'm limited edition.

## ON FORTUNATE MISFORTUNES

Right when I'm on a roll, Lady Fortune shows up, and my momentum comes to a screeching halt. Eh, like this one time, Jessie was about to be evicted from his apartment because he failed to pay the rent. His minimum-wage job was nothing to brag about either—and he happened to lose it and his rent-sharing roommate. Down on his luck, off he goes all bundled up one winter morning to a job interview. Jessie was in no mood for bad weather complicating his drive to his very important opportunity. Now, I happen to live for moments like these. See, I showed up again and sent him some transmission trouble. Jessie wasn't the only one whining—his car started whining too. In seconds, his used two-seater roadster chugged to a full stop on the shoulder. Jessie jumped out of his car, kicked the tire, and pulled out a good chunk of his hair, cursing every second in between. His job interview went up in smoke. As he sat streaming tears in the front seat, he discovered from his phone that just ten miles ahead of him, black ice had caused a sixty-five-car pileup, one that sent two dozen drivers to the hospital. Diesel fuel had spilled onto the highway too. As vehicles uncontrollably skidded on the black ice and crashed, the fuel exploded, taking the lives of many more. Suddenly, Jessie was no longer an unhappy guy. And all it took was one last visit from me for Jessie to feel grateful to be alive. Oh, and Lady Fortune had his job interview rescheduled. This is what I call a fortunate misfortune. Admit it, the complex way I work is not so terrible, is it?

## ON GETTING A RAW DEAL

Raw deal? You're calling the challenges, hardship, and misery I dole out *raw*? As in raw red kidney beans or raw bitter almonds or raw wild mushrooms—none of which should ever be consumed raw, by the way. Or even raw data or raw materials? Indeed, I'm quite aware that information is more valuable than . . . *raw* data and that finished products are far more desirable than . . . *raw* materials. But me—a raw deal? I'm having a little hissy fit here! Commiserate with me, and come up with something more deferential. You might as well call me *crude* or *unrefined* or even *unprocessed*. Just like a so-called raw deal, raw goods can be transformed, with the right approach, into something incredibly useful, even delicious. Ever have sautéed wild mushrooms, with a little garlic and black pepper? Delish! Raw materials have value, because without them, you wouldn't end up with the finished goods. Listen, I may not hand out sunshine and rainbows, but I am petrified you'd consider my offerings to have nothing more than the harshness of a *raw deal* of all things. I'm more beneficial than that. Hmph!

## ON DEFEAT

I know you feel defeated, like the Egyptian Mamluk soldiers by Napoleon at the Battle of the Pyramids or the Vikings by the armies of Wessex or the pasture-raised Thanksgiving turkey by the local turkey farm. But defeat is just a temporary state of being—unless you're the Thanksgiving bird, which is, by the way, pardoned annually by the highest office in the nation. But getting back on track. Defeat is hardly considered a permanent condition unless you surrender—and even then, it's subject to interpretation. Sometimes the clear winner is the one who puts up the bravest fight. Overwhelming as it is, the struggle I lay claim to has limits in its ability to weaken you; in many cases, the setbacks I deliver motivate the crushed to become, surprisingly, mightier, and, therefore uncrushed, like sea salt—which is actually thought to bring prosperity. So harness the disappointments and use them in a more productive way. Generally, I suggest assuming the nature of water: supple enough to withstand any attack from yours truly—except for the electrical type, for obvious reasons.

## ON HIS DYING DAY

It's hard to please all of the people all of the time.
See, eighty-five-year-old Dan had been ailing for
days. He lay in his bed surrounded by his daughters,
granddaughters, great-granddaughters, their husbands,
and his ten-year-old wild-striped tabby cat. Dan told
them, "I don't want to go. I've lived a great life." His
family looked upon him with sad eyes. What could
they do? So in the middle of the night, I came around
and whisked him away. In heaven, guess who else but
Lady Fortune showed up to greet good ol' Dan? She
introduced him to his seven golf courses green as
emeralds, his fiery-red sports convertible, his three-

story mansion, and his lake-size pool. Dan looked around with his jaw dropped practically to the clouds upon which he stood. As his neck twisted to absorb the majesty that was now his, he furrowed his brows, turned beet red in the face, and scowled like he'd never scowled in all his eighty-five years on earth. Lady Fortune asked him what in heaven was the matter. Dan replied, "I waited eighty-five years to arrive here? I thought I had it good before." Irked to no end, Dan twisted his frail body, then yelled at Lady Fortune with all the vehemence of a dejected aged man, "And you couldn't have brought me here any sooner?" Eh, no one is ever happy with either of us, are they?

Thank you for reading *In Defense of Misfortune*.
If you enjoyed this collection of humorous essays,
please consider leaving a review at your favorite
retailer and helping other readers discover surprisingly
entertaining books of humor.

Books in the In Defense Of series
*In Defense of Babyhood*
*In Defense of the Grim Reaper*
*In Defense of Seniorhood*

Visit my author website
www.riyapresents.com